From Crackers to Coal Oil

A gun in the schoolroom leads to romance and marriage.

**The Early History of Sunland, California
Volume 4**

ML Tiernan

From Crackers to Coal Oil

www.maryleetiernan.com
Second printing April 1, 2015
10 9 8 7 6 5 4 3 2

ISBN 978-0983067238 (Paperback)

©1999 ©2010 Mary Lee Tiernan. All rights reserved. No portion of this product may be photographed, scanned, translated, reproduced, copied, or reduced to any tangible or electronic medium or machine-readable form, without the prior written consent of Mary Lee Tiernan.

Photograph on cover courtesy of Bolton Hall Museum, Tujunga, California.
Quote on cover is from an interview with the Rowleys.

Contents

Trouble in the Schoolroom 5

A New Teacher 7

Loron Rowley 9

The Rowley Family 13

Back to Town 21

Footnotes 28

Bibliography 29

The Early History of Sunland, California series 31

Author's Notes

The researcher, like a detective, examines the evidence to try to determine the real story. Unfortunately for researchers, we cannot re-examine witnesses or revisit scenes because in most cases, they have long since disappeared. So we sort through the conflicting data to find the most reliable and logical explanations. I have done my best to follow the clues and weave as authentic a story as possible.

My thanks to the staff at Bolton Hall Museum, Tujunga, California for their assistance with this project.

Trouble in the Schoolroom

A mid-year crisis in the schoolroom! It was not the usual problem of rain swelling the Big Tujunga River, thus making the road across the wash impassable. With so few families in Sunland, the children attended the original school built in 1888 in Little Tujunga, or Tujunga Terrace[1],

The original schoolhouse in Little Tujunga, or Tujunga Terrace, later named Lake View Terrace. Photo courtesy of Bolton Hall Museum.

later renamed Lake View Terrace.

Any heavy rain prevented travel on the dirt roads in Sunland, which were really little more than narrow passages with two ruts worn from wagon wheels. The road across the wash completely flooded, ensuring the children a day off from school.

This time the crisis came from within the school itself. Pioneer children led the same rugged life as their parents who were carving a living out of harsh land. They often walked miles to and from school. The boys sometimes carried guns to shoot jackrabbits for sport, or to kill deadly snakes for safety. The young schoolmaster, apparently not used to the boys' rough ways and wanting to establish stricter discipline, cut willow switches and brought them to school. He laid them on his desk as a warning against their antics. In turn, one of the boys pulled out his knife and another his gun, and imitating the teacher, placed the weapons on their desks.

On the way home from school that day, the teacher heard shots and felt the wind from the bullets as they whistled by his ears. Although a contemporary claimed it was just "the boys having good clean fun,"[2] the schoolmaster quit. Without a teacher, the bell no longer rang in the morning to summon the children to the one-room schoolhouse.

A New Teacher

By 1891, Loron Thomas Rowley[3] played a central role in anything that happened in the village of Sunland. He immediately wrote to his brother Quintin, a doctor living in Downey, inquiring about a candidate to replace the schoolmaster. In reply, Quintin sent twenty-one-year-old Virginia Florence Newcomb, graduate of the Normal School in Los Angeles.[4]

Born the same year her parents arrived from Mississippi to help establish the town of Downey, Virginia knew the difficulties of pioneer life in a struggling village. She walked into the same situation as her predecessor, but better prepared. As a younger child in a large family of boys, years of dealing with her brothers would help her handle Sunland's youth. Her father, a sergeant who fought during the Civil War under General Robert E. Lee, also advised her on how to deal with the 'upstarts.' With Virginia, order returned to the schoolroom.

Loron helped Virginia settle in—and more. While she taught for the next two years, he also courted her. The ten years' difference in their ages mattered little to either of them. When they married in 1893, he brought her to his homestead in an area in Tujunga later named Seven Hills.

Springs from the mountain provided her new home in Rowley Canyon with plenty of water for home, garden, and crops, at least for most of the year. Only in late summer did the flow of water cease. The blessings of plentiful water outweighed the problems of living in the canyon—the boulders that crashed down during the rain or the coyotes that howled through the night from their dens in the wash.

The first one-room schoolhouse in Sunland located in Sunland Park. Photo courtesy of Mrs. Elizabeth Schell.

Loron Rowley

For both Loron and Virginia, the greatest drawback to pioneer life was not having enough time to read. Like his wife, Loron was well-educated. He loved to quote from Homer's *Iliad* and recite the works of his favorite poet, Robert Burns, imitating Burns' Scottish dialect. Loren's education had come to an abrupt end during his senior year at the University of Minnesota.

The depression in the Midwest after the Civil War forced many farmers to abandon their land and migrate. Loron's family also sought to escape starving conditions. Colorful brochures and posters published by the railroads promised a high yield of land for farming in the glorious climate of California. That, combined with the low rail-rates, prompted Loron to leave Minnesota and scout for government land where the family could re-establish itself.

Loron joined the flow of migrants and boarded the Southern Pacific for points west.[5] During his first year in California, Loron joined two uncles who lived in Mandeville Canyon, raising bees and selling honey. While learning the in's and out's of this profitable business, he kept his ears open for news about government land available for homesteading. In 1882, he found such land in the Monte Vista Valley. So he loaded some hives into a buckboard, drove up through Glendale, pitched a tent, and homesteaded 160 acres. With the help of the Verdugo family[6], he built a ranch house.

Despite its 'failure' during the land boom, the village of farmers continued to grow. Photo courtesy of Bolton Hall Museum.

Besides establishing his beehives and raising cattle, Loron marketed the wood he chopped on the ranch by carting it out of the canyon on sleds and transporting it by wagon into Los Angeles. Few people lived in the valley at that time, before the impending Land Boom, because the poor roads—or lack of them—discouraged settlement. For the woodcutters, however, Monte Vista Valley furnished a lucrative business. Los Angles needed wood as fuel for cooking and heating. The abundant supply of native greasewood and pine trees that grew along the fringes of the mountains and in the canyons quite literally went up in smoke in L.A. By the 1890s, the denuded forests would need replanting.

While Loron struggled to raise cattle and keep the beehives productive, the developers arrived. At first, he hired on as a construction worker, but seeing the need for supplies for the workers, he contracted with the promoters in 1885 to build a two-story structure on the southwest corner of Central Avenue and First Street (later Fenwick and Oro Vista) for mail distribution and a general store which sold everything from crackers to coal oil. Loron would go by wagon to L.A. to buy supplies, stay overnight, and come back the next day.

Most of the mail, which Loron picked up at the Roscoe train station, came for workmen building the Monte Vista Hotel. When the Land Boom collapsed in 1888, many of the original land purchasers disappeared, as did much of Loron's business. During this period, Virginia arrived to teach school. After they married, Virginia shared the growing pains of Loron's enterprises while they continued to develop the ranch and began raising a family with the birth of their son Eustace in 1896.

Although Loron was ill-suited for rough work because

a bout with typhoid fever in his youth left him with troublesome legs, the needs of his family outweighed his own personal problems. When he'd established himself in the valley, he sent for the family. His father Asa joined him around 1888 and homesteaded land adjacent to Loron's. His sister Mary Grace followed shortly thereafter and staked her land south of theirs. Loron and his father continued with the productive bees, but changed from cattle to planting olive groves, peach orchards, and alfalfa. The three Rowley homesteads covered much of the land from Big Tujunga Canyon along the base of the mountain towards La Crescenta. With land they bought or quitclaimed in the ensuing years, the family ended up owning over 1,000 acres.

The Rowley Family

When the promoter Frank H. Barclay lost his land in the demise of the Land Boom, he also lost the Monte Vista Hotel. The hotel remained vacant into the 1890s, when Loron's brother Quintin bought it as an investment. He persuaded Loron and Virginia to move into the hotel to guard his investment. Here their second son Robert (1898)

Robert and Eustace Rowley (back) with their Aunt Marion. Most roads In Sunland were little more than narrow passages with two ruts worn from wagon wheels. Photo courtesy of Bolton Hall Museum.

and their first daughter Dorothy (1902) were born. Virginia had her hands full with the adventurous Robert. He liked to climb on the balconies, chase bats out from the belfry, and race his bike around the porch that encircled the hotel. Once he climbed up on the roof to slide down, nearly killing himself.

Lack of medical care in the valley made accidents or illness a very serious threat. Midwives delivered children, or at least attended to the mother until a doctor could arrive. Many births were never recorded. Imagine the irony these children experienced later in life having to prove they existed before they could get a birth certificate.

A family often had to seek medical assistance outside the valley. When Dorothy Rowley fell off Jenny Wornum's horse and broke her arm, her parents had to race four and a half miles through the rain to the train depot and then wait to flag down the next train to reach Burbank where a doctor could set her arm. How agonizing must those hours have been for both the injured Dorothy and her anxious parents. Before modern medicines, such as antibiotics, even a doctor could not ensure a cure for ailments that today may seem commonplace. The youngest Rowley, Clara Virginia, would die at age 14 from an ear infection.

Often pioneers either suffered through an ailment or depended on home remedies. Virginia insisted on serving her 'Senna tea' as a prescription for every affliction, be it a headache or a stomach ache. When a neighbor fell sick, Virginia could be counted on to appear with some of her tea. She served it both internally as a purge, or externally, as a poultice soaked in tea water with turpentine as the equivalent of an antibiotic.

Ranchers did continue to buy large acreage in the valley during the 1880s and 1890s. They planted orchards, vineyards, and olive groves on the lower side of the valley, where water was available. The ever-industrious Loron began hauling this produce from the valley—grapes, oranges, lemons—first in his wagon, then by truck, and established the first freight line in the valley. Some of the ranch owners did not live on the land themselves, but hired

Wentworth Ave. looking toward Sherman Grove Ave.
The slope of the road caused flooding during rains.
Photo courtesy of Bolton Hall Museum.

others to work it. This brought in additional families who supported the store and post office and the eventual opening of Sunland's own school.

By 1900 Loron operated the store and the ranch and his hauling business, but another down-market made money tight. A job opened in the newly formed government Forest Service, which reforested mountains that had burned or been denuded by the woodcutters. So Loron became Sunland's first forest ranger. With all his enterprises, Loron needed help. Virginia stepped in and became the first postmistress of Sunland, a position she kept until 1908. When Mrs. Huse replaced Virginia as postmistress, she, too, worked another job—as correspondent for the Glendale newspaper. She wrote a column once a week about news she gleaned by reading the postcards that came and went in the mail.

The children, too, did their part to help. When Loron began hauling produce by truck from the valley to Los Angeles, the uncooperative Cadillac often broke down. Since he couldn't repair it himself, he hitched a horse to it to pull it all the way to a garage in Burbank. Intrigued by the engine, as boys often are, Robert began tinkering with it until he learned to fix it, saving his father both time and money. Sometimes, however, Robert and the other village boys used their knowledge of cars a bit deviously. Breakdowns being common, when Dr. Speighs's car refused to start after church, he thought little of giving the boys 50 cents to start it for him. What would he have thought if he knew that while he was in church, the boys disconnected a part, and then simply reconnected it, to earn their 50 cents?

Virginia insisted on education for her children, rudimentary as it might be in a one-room school, where lessons focused on 'the three R's,' geography, and spelling. Missing school every time the river swelled from rain and wiped out the road interfered with those lessons.

Community picnic in Sunland Park. The park was the center of community social activities: picnics, sports, and holiday festivities, including a parade on July 4th.
Photo courtesy of Bolton Hall Museum.

The children may not have minded, but Virginia did. To circumvent the problem, the Rowleys helped start a new school, right in the center of town—in the park.[7] The new Sunland School, however, soon ran into another problem. To qualify for county money, six children needed to attend the school. One year, attendance fell to five. Not to be defeated by such regulations, Virginia enrolled her second son, Robert, at age four and a half, as the sixth child.

When Quintin Rowley sold the Monte Vista Hotel in 1903, the family moved back to the ranch house in Seven Hills. From there, the boys walked two miles to school. To amuse themselves on the way, they sometimes brought along the family's 12-guage Winchester pump gun to shoot rabbits for target practice. After the incident that had originally brought Virginia to Sunland, the policy about guns in school—and discipline in general—had changed. The boys hid the gun before entering school so the teacher wouldn't take it away from them. Their teacher kept a firm hand on his students. If they misbehaved, he'd crack their fingers. But sometimes students enjoy a little payback. Once, when the class went to the pasture to collect mistletoe, the teacher got caught in a bog. The kids heard his cries, but just let him stew for a while before coming to his rescue.

Living in an area known for its hunting of deer, dove, and quail, it was not unusual for local boys to develop an avid interest in the sport. When son Robert insisted at too early an age to go hunting with his uncles, Virginia's experience with handling boys served her well. Concerned with his safety, yet not wanting to crush his spirits, Virginia allowed her son to discover the truth for himself. She placed a shotgun in his hands. When Robert fired, the recoil knocked him over backwards. The day he could fire the gun without being knocked over, Virginia allowed Robert to join the hunting parties.

The new, enlarged Sunland School when it moved from Sunland Park to Hillrose Street. Photo courtesy of Marshall Murray.

Shooting was more than a sport for early settlers. Even the women and kids learned to shoot for protection. Whether trudging through miles of sagebrush and cactus on a hike or horseback ride, or on the way to swimming holes in the Big Tujunga wash, they often ran into rattlesnakes along the way. And the canyons still teemed with wildlife. Although Virginia cooped her chickens to protect them, the coyotes still managed to steal into the hen house at night. In years to come, her boys would jump out of bed and grab their guns during the ruckus of a raid, with hopes of killing a coyote as they chased them off.

Hunting put meat on the table. Individuals shot jackrabbits and quail for family dinners, but when someone shot big game, the whole town came to carve it up and share the spoils. The first time thirteen-year-old Robert shot a deer, he proudly tried to imitate the men and lift it onto his shoulders, but failed. The deer weighed five pounds more than he did. The Rowley brothers often brought deer back from their hunting trips to the canyon and shared the meat with neighbors. To keep meat from spoiling, Virginia covered it with gunny sacks, kept wet with water, to keep it cool.

Back to Town

With business centered in town and the boys in school, living out on the ranch proved difficult at times. So in 1905, the Rowleys built the first rock house in Sunland on Hill Street near Flower Avenue (later Hillrose and Floralita). The backyard accommodated Virginia's flock of chickens and her vegetable garden. In the pasture next to

Sunland store circa 1913, believed to the Rowleys'.
Photo courtesy of Bolton Hall Museum.

the house, where running water from a spring kept grass growing all year on the damp ground, the family kept horses and milking cows. Virginia taught each of her children to milk the cows as soon as they were old enough to carry a bucket. As they grew, they were also expected to help in the store.

Once Marion forgot she was supposed to be tending the store and went off with her friends instead. A customer came, needing a pan. Finding no one to wait on her, she helped herself and left a note explaining what she had done: "I left 25 cents. Thought that about right. If not, let me know."[8] Luckily for Marion, stealing, either the merchandise or the money in the cash register, did not fit the pioneer character. They all worked too hard and respected one another's efforts.

The kitchen stove and two fireplaces in the new home kept the downstairs well-heated during cold weather. But upstairs, the bedrooms remained cold. At night, the children went to bed with a rock, inscribed with their name, which had been warmed in the fireplace. They wrapped the rock in old newspaper and put it in the bed to keep their feet warm. Since Smuggle, their cat, did not have a personal rock, she just crawled right into the fireplace to keep warm—and usually walked around with slightly singed fur.

Virginia counted on Sunday to bring the family

together after a hectic week. After services at the Free Methodist Church, she picked a hen no longer laying eggs, and the boys killed it for their traditional chicken-and-dumplings family dinner. She gathered beans, carrots, and other vegetables from her garden and made biscuits and cornbread. Their peach orchards provided fruit, fresh or preserved, depending on the season. After a hearty mid-day meal, Sunday night light supper consisted of a mixture of honey and butter poured over hot biscuits and more peaches. Virginia's daughter Dorothy later regretted never being able to duplicate dumplings as delectable as those her mother made.

The Rowleys built one of the first rock houses in Sunland, on Hillrose near Floralita. Photo courtesy of Bolton Hall Museum.

Claims about Sunland's clean, healthy air must have had some validity. In spite of Virginia's hectic schedule keeping two homes—the ranch and the newer house on Hillrose—cooking, raising chickens, and growing vegetables, and her job as postmistress and mother of five, and her husband's enterprises with the general store, forestry service, orchards, and newer delivery service of groceries, newspapers, and milk to farms and families in the now developing town of Tujunga, the family still found time to gather in the evenings on the front porch, where the children played jacks or practiced their musical instruments.

The Rowley house in 1999.

Each member of the family showed musical ability, and Virginia insisted the children take music lessons from Walter Maygrove, the local music virtuoso. Although music primarily served as family entertainment, when Bolton Hall opened in Tujunga, Virginia, Loron, and Eustace played for the Saturday night dances: folk and square dances or Virginia reels for the older generation; waltzes and the two-step for the younger.

Regardless of how much the family liked living in town and being together, they could not entirely vacate the ranch. Families continued to move into the valley. Some bought land; some quitclaimed deeds. A person could quitclaim land by occupying it and paying taxes for over five years, then go to court and claim it, even though someone else might hold papers. The paper holder had to pay taxes, work on the land or live on it, to retain ownership. Many of the people who had bought land from Barclay during the Land Boom did not occupy the land. Worse, they had been given unrecorded deeds from an unrecorded lithograph map, which didn't have much value in court. Some parcels of the same land had been sold several times. It took 20 years of lawsuits to straighten out who owned what.

The Rowleys themselves took advantage of the quitclaim process and acquired more land in town. But they also feared that someone might try to quitclaim their homestead. Virginia often stayed at the ranch with her youngest daughters, Marion (born 1906) and Clara Virginia (born 1908). Without other means available, the family invented their own system of communication. At a prearranged hour, Virginia waved a lantern to signal the family below that she and the girls were okay.

When Eustace and Robert finished elementary school, they went to Burbank High School. They hitched a ride with the buggy on the mail run to Roscoe Station at 5:50, caught the train at 6:00, and arrived in Burbank before school opened. On the way home, however, they walked the five miles uphill to get home. For Robert's second year, the boys switched to the smaller, but closer, San Fernando High. Their father gave them a horse and buggy to drive the 10 miles to school; a barn in the yard provided shelter for the horse during the day. Robert's graduating class in 1915 consisted of 17 students. Although the boys managed the difficult trek to school, Virginia felt the route too demanding for her daughters.

In 1918, the family moved to Glendale so Dorothy, Marion, and Clara Virginia could attend Glendale High School. Two years later, Virginia's cousin William Nance bought the general store, and Loron became a truant officer for the Glendale School District. The family sold off their land. In 1922, James T. Fitzgerald bought the 160-acre homestead in Seven Hills for $24,000. During the Great

Depression, Robert sold some of the acreage in town; after World War II, he sold what remained.

The Rowley family may be gone from Sunland, but they have left traces of their presence. Their namesakes—Rowley Canyon and Rowley Place in Seven Hills—bear witness to these early settlers. Their house at 8436 Hillrose is occupied by another family who, fortunately, has preserved one of Sunland's earliest landmarks.

#####

Footnotes

[1] When the colony of Little Lands decided to rename itself and call the town Tujunga, it caused confusion because Little Tujunga—later Lake View Terrace—already existed. Old timers were both amused and annoyed by the repetition of the name.

[2] Rowley, Robert. *Sunland-Tujunga.*

[3] Loron Thomas Rowley: born June 3, 1860 – died May 31, 1942.

[4] Virginia Florence Newcomb Rowley: born 1870 – died March 1938. A Normal School was an institute for training teachers.

[5] For a description of traveling accommodations on the trains and the railroad price-fare wars, see *Volume 1, Hotels of the Hopeful.*

[6] The Verdugo family's Mexican land grant included parts of Glendale, La Crescenta, and La Canada.

[7] The school was probably located in the northeast corner of Sunland Park.

[8] Personal interview with Marion Rowley by Charles Miller.

Bibliography

"Blumfields Have Resided in Same House on Sherman Grove Since 1906 Marriage." *The Record-Ledger*, September 30, 1954.

"Born at Old Monte Vista Hotel, Speaker Revives Past of Area." *The Record-Ledger*, February 11, 1971.

Colville, Lucy. "Rowley Recalls Early Days of Sunland-Tujunga." *The Record-Ledger*, September, 1973.

"First School in the Sunland Tujunga Valley." *The Record-Ledger*, Historical & Progress Edition, May 21, 1953.

"First Sunland School Founded about 1898 in 1-Room Building." *The Record-Ledger*, Historical & Progress Edition, May 21, 1953.

Lombard, Sarah. "Monte Vista = Sunland." *The Record-Ledger*, September 22, 1977.

Lombard, Sarah. "Verdant Valley Attracts Settlers." *The Record-Ledger*, October 13, 1977.

"Public School, Monte Vista." *The Record-Ledger*, Historical & Progress Edition, May 21, 1953.

Rowley, Dorothy. Personal interview by Joan Conrad, Viola Carlson, and Mary Lou Pozzo. February 17, 1996.

Rowley, Marion. Personal interview by Charles Miller. June 27, 1986.

Rowley, Robert. Personal interview by Viola Carlson. 1974.

Rowley, Robert. *Sunland-Tujunga*.

"Sunland School Nears 70 Years at Same Site." *The Record-Ledger*, July 3, 1975.

Sunland-Tujunga: Nestled between the Verdugo Hills and the San Gabriel Mts. The Sunland-Tujunga Chamber of Commerce, March, 1947.

The Early History of Sunland, California

8 Volume Series
Also available as ebooks

Vol. 1 *Hotels for the Hopeful* Land promoters of the 1880s promised a perfect life of health, wealth, and pleasure. Although their promises fell short of reality, the village did grow and prosper in the hands of farmers.

Vol. 2 *The Roscoe Robbers and the Sensational Train Robbery of 1894* Two robbers posed as passengers to flag down the train. When the engineer recognized danger, he opened the throttle and sped past. The bandits threw the spur switch, and the train careened full speed off the tracks.

Vol. 3 *The Parson and His Cemetery* Parson Wornum was so loved that when he died, the whole village attended his funeral. Years of neglect of his cemetery spelled disaster in 1978 when heavy rains tore open graves and washed bodies down the hillside.

Vol. 4 ***From Crackers to Coal Oil*** When a student pulled out his gun and laid it on his desk, the tiny one-room school found itself needing a new teacher. That brought Virginia Newcomb, a romance, and a new family that helped to develop the town, leaving behind a detailed account of pioneer life in a small village.

Vol. 5 ***He Never Came Home*** Joe Ardizzone, a local grape-grower, doubled as a hit-man for the Mafia. During Prohibition, Joe's bootlegging activities caught him in the middle of in-house quarreling. In 1931, he left on a short trip and disappeared into the pages of history.

Vol. 6 ***Lancasters Lake*** When Edgar Lancaster dredged the swamp on his land, he created a lake which became a treasured landmark. For 25 years, visitors flocked to its cool shores, and Hollywood used the lake as a set location for some of its early movies.

Vol. 7 ***Living in Big Tujunga Canyon*** Early settlers, like the Johnson family, found their way into the canyon, a dense woodland bristling with wildlife. 50 years later, the Webber family faced the wrath of the river now winding down a denuded mountainside.

Vol. 8 *From Whence They Came* The Land Boom of the 1880s brought immigrants from around the world. Two generations of Blumfields survived the difficulties of farming and water shortages through industry and imagination.

www.ingramcontent.com/pod-product-compliance
Lightning Source LLC
Chambersburg PA
CBHW061349040426
42444CB00011B/3152